# Noses

## Are for Picking

## THE SENSE OF SMELL

### Katherine Hengel

Consulting Editor, Diane Craig, M.A./Reading Specialist

A Division of ABDO

**ABDO**
Publishing Company

# visit us at www.abdopublishing.com

Published by ABDO Publishing Company, a division of ABDO, P.O. Box 398166, Minneapolis, Minnesota 55439. Copyright © 2012 by Abdo Consulting Group, Inc. International copyrights reserved in all countries. No part of this book may be reproduced in any form without written permission from the publisher. SandCastle™ is a trademark and logo of ABDO Publishing Company.

Printed in the United States of America, North Mankato, Minnesota
102011
012012

 PRINTED ON RECYCLED PAPER

Editor: Liz Salzmann
Content Developer: Nancy Tuminelly
Cover and Interior Design and Production: Oona Gaarder-Juntti, Mighty Media, Inc.
Photo Credits: BananaStock, Digital Vision, Jupiterimages, Medioimages, Photodisc, Shutterstock, Thinkstock

**Library of Congress Cataloging-in-Publication Data**
Hengel, Katherine.
  Noses are for picking : the sense of smell / Katherine Hengel.
    p. cm. -- (All about your senses)
  ISBN 978-1-61783-200-0
  1. Nose--Juvenile literature. 2. Senses and sensation--Juvenile literature. I. Title.
  QP458.H36 2012
  612.2'3--dc23
                          2011023495

## SandCastle™ Level: Transitional

SandCastle™ books are created by a team of professional educators, reading specialists, and content developers around five essential components—phonemic awareness, phonics, vocabulary, text comprehension, and fluency—to assist young readers as they develop reading skills and strategies and increase their general knowledge. All books are written, reviewed, and leveled for guided reading, early reading intervention, and Accelerated Reader® programs for use in shared, guided, and independent reading and writing activities to support a balanced approach to literacy instruction. The SandCastle™ series has four levels that correspond to early literacy development. The levels are provided to help teachers and parents select appropriate books for young readers.

| Emerging Readers | Beginning Readers | Transitional Readers | Fluent Readers |
| (no flags) | (1 flag) | (2 flags) | (3 flags) |

# Table of Contents

# Noses

## Are for Picking

Noses are special. They can do a lot! Robert puts his finger in his nose. He thinks a bug got up there!

**What else are noses for? What can noses sense?**

# Noses

## Are for Smelling

Colleen smells a flower. She likes the way it smells! It **reminds** her of her Aunt Melanie's perfume.

When we breathe, odors go into our noses. The odors float up to **sense receptors**. The receptors send messages to our brains. That's how we smell things!

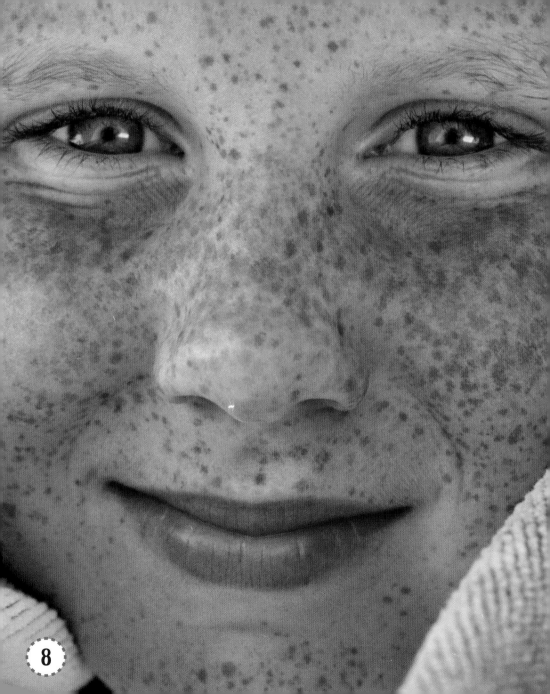

# Our Sense of Smell

Our noses help us sense the world around us. Sensing with our noses is called smelling. Smell is one of our five senses.

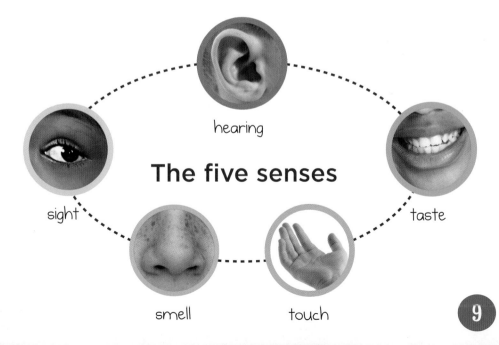

**The five senses**

hearing

sight

taste

smell

touch

# Noses

## Are for Cooking

Susan can smell her waffle **toasting**. It might be done! She doesn't want to burn it.

# Noses

## Are for Stinks

Henry just got done running. He takes his shoes off. They smell really stinky. His mom and dad agree!

Everyone's sense of smell is a little different. Something can smell good to one person. But someone else might think it smells bad. It all depends on your sense of smell!

# Noses

## Are for Breathing

Our noses smell things all the time. They also **filter** the air we breathe. Tiny hairs in our noses trap dirt and dust.

Noses can do a lot!
What else are noses for?

# Noses

## Are for Plugging

Mary thinks the trash smells awful! Her brother was supposed to take it out. But he forgot! Mary **plugs** her nose. Odors can't get in now! She won't have to smell the trash!

# Noses

## Are for Blowing

Becky has to blow her nose. She has **allergies**. They act up in the spring. That's when Becky uses a lot of **tissues**!

# Noses

## Are for Eskimo Kisses

Nathan loves his mom. They give each other Eskimo kisses. Nathan thinks Eskimo kisses are fun!

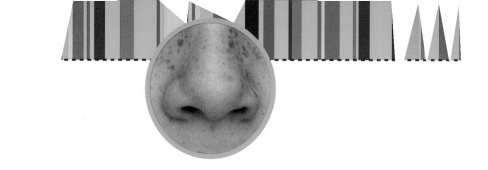

# Facts About Smell

◆ Noses can smell between 4,000 and 10,000 different **scents**!

◆ We are better at remembering smells than pictures.

◆ Noses can tell where scents come from! We can follow an odor to its **source**.

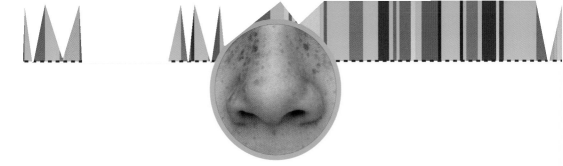

# Smell Quiz

1. When we breathe, odors go into our noses. True or false?

2. Smelling is one of our five senses. True or false?

3. Everyone's sense of smell is the same. True or false?

4. Our noses do not **filter** the air we breathe. True or false?

# Glossary

**allergy** – sickness caused by touching, breathing, or eating certain things.

**filter** – to clean air by passing it through something that removes any dirt from it.

**plug** – to close or fill an opening.

**sense receptor** – one of the tiny parts of the body that senses things, such as odors, and sends the information to the brain.

**source** – the point where something comes from or begins.

**tissue** – a thin paper used to wipe one's face or blow one's nose.

**toast** – to cook something, such as bread, until it is dry and brown.